D1345445

Ethna MacCarthy
POEMS

Ethna MacCarthy
POEMS

Edited by EOIN O'BRIEN and GERALD DAWE

WITHDRAWN FROM STOCK

THE LILLIPUT PRESS
DUBLIN

First published 2019 by
THE LILLIPUT PRESS
62–63 Sitric Road, Arbour Hill
Dublin 7, Ireland
www.lilliputpress.ie

Frontispiece: Garrity, Devin A. (Ed.), *New Irish Poets*
(New York: Devin-Adair, 1948).

ISBN 9781843517696

A CIP record for this title is available from
The British Library.

1 3 5 7 9 10 8 6 4 2

The Lilliput Press gratefully acknowledges the financial
support of the Arts Council/An Chomhairle Ealaíon.

Set in 12pt on 15.4pt Centaur by Marsha Swan
Printed in Poland by Drukarnia Skelniarz

CONTENTS

INTRODUCTION

I

Dr Ethna MacCarthy, born in Coleraine, County Londonderry, in 1903, was brought up in an upper-middle-class Catholic family in south County Dublin, although her mother was Protestant; a background steeped in literary and cultural connections spanning the generations and the social milieu of Dublin and London life. Her father, Brendan MacCarthy, was an eminent doctor whose speciality was public health; her grandfather was the distinguished writer Denis Florence MacCarthy, and her aunt, Sister Mary Stanislaus MacCarthy, was also a poet. MacCarthy, a fascinating woman, scholar and physician, who crossed many boundaries, emerges as a writer of impressive achievement. Her life was tragically cut short by illness: she died of throat cancer in May 1959 at the age of fifty-six.

Perhaps best known to posterity through her association with Samuel Beckett – as one of his earliest loves, commemorated in significant writing of his, including early poems such as 'Alba', fiction including 'A Wet Night' and *Dream of Fair to Middling Women,* and the play *Krapp's Last Tape* – Ethna MacCarthy deserves to be better understood in her own right.

As an important and creative part of a cosmopolitan and free-thinking generation in post-Independence Dublin, which included poets such as Leslie Daiken, Patrick MacDonogh, Eileen Shanahan and Rhoda Coghill, MacCarthy was a Scholar and a First-Class Moderator (1926) at Trinity College Dublin. Like other friends of hers, such as Beckett himself and his dear friend and confidant A.J. Leventhal, whom she would eventually marry in 1956, MacCarthy taught languages at the university in the 1930s and 40s before studying medicine, which she practised in Dublin and in the East End of London. This dual life of literature and languages and medicine has a long and productive tradition in Irish cultural life going back to the eighteenth century and includes, most famously, the Wilde family. (See, for example, Davis Coakley, *The Importance of Being Irish* and Eoin O'Brien, *The Weight of Compassion and other essays.*)

Denis Johnston, the Irish playwright and broadcaster, who knew MacCarthy well in 1920s Dublin, remarked: 'She has never been shy, can be frank, and outspoken to a degree, is absolutely fearless, intolerant of mediocrity and finds it difficult to suffer fools gladly.' Precious wonder that writers were drawn to her energy and independence, qualities that are present in the poems gathered here for the first time. The poems have been reproduced as far as possible as they appear in Ethna MacCarthy's original journal.

*

MacCarthy's life in Dublin is an obvious starting point since the city features in many of the poems: Grafton Street, Dublin Castle, the Provost's House (Trinity College) along with an inner-city life seen through the prism of a T.S. Eliot-like lens, here in 'Lullaby':

There is no moon, for fog and damp
submerge the city
and giant cobwebs hang
from lamp to lamp.
The river out of pity
smuggles decently
its pauper cargo
shrouded in mist
past the Customs
out to sea.

There is also the hint of the south side of the bay, likely drawing upon her growing up and adult life in Sandymount in 'Desmond' on Sandymount Avenue, with the marsh and strand, bird life, churches and convent all forming a backdrop to several poems, including 'Frost':

Tinsel rain
on the window pane,
blue snow
on the road below,
tangerine glow
from curtained casements
the tenting of the sky swings low.

So too MacCarthy's 'double life' as a scholar of romance languages and literatures can be seen in the early influences of Spanish popular song, ballad and classical myth alongside the subject matter of MacCarthy's hospital experience. In poems such as 'The Theatre' and 'Viaticum' – discussed later along with 'The Charity' – the poet directly links her professional life as a doctor to her place as a poet. 'This commemorative ode', she explains in a subtitle to 'The Charity', 'was spoken ... in connection with the Bi-Centenary of the Rotunda Hospital' (see note on p. 59).

There is, however, a deeper and more challenging side to MacCarthy's achievement as a poet. From the earliest of the poems written in the mid-1930s, when she was herself in her early thirties, to the work published in her final decade, the conflicting strains of an emotional energy seem caught up in the conventional and performative aspects of her life. This can, on the one hand, express itself in a mocking tone, as in 'The Theatre':

> I seem to sway
> holding this tray
> waiting and waiting
> (what *did* the sister say?)

On the other hand, the myths and fables of her literary reading come into a personal questioning focus particularly in poems set elsewhere, such as 'Barcelona':

> The cloth and the fish
> and the grapes were white
> but the mariners were eating meat
> and laughed and talked in a tongue I knew
> but could not understand
> for the blankness in my head.
> Where now is your ship mariner
> and what was it you said?

The deft assonantal rhymes – white / meat; understand / head / said – characterize much of the poetry with its dramatic voices' compression. But what is most impressive is the manner in which MacCarthy brings surprise and the unexpected into her work, in 'Song' for example, with its 'fairy coach / of sparkling glass':

and dark the road we must traverse,
that crystal coach a lamplit hearse.

In 'Untitled', too, the injunction '… let us live alone / and drink each other in a cup / that has no past or future to discuss' conveys a recurring impatience with reason and the rational. An everyday scene of 'washing on the line' is transformed into something 'grotesque' as 'they freeze in tortured attitudes / paralysed by Winter in their sin / and rigor mortis has set in' ('Frost'). While the birds in 'The Migrants' — curlews, wild geese, swans — are reimagined and seen in a Dante-like landscape 'thrusting their desolate image / ghost voices shaking the air / in warning and fear', as well they might in 1948:

> the migrants bitter accusatory cry
> 'we want that you too might not die'[.]

'The Migrants' is a powerful poem by any standards. It was in the mid- to late 1940s that MacCarthy hit her stride as a poet with several very moving and self-confident poems. The decade sees the writing of 'Lullaby', a truly remarkable poem, which foreshadows the exposed lunar and death-haunted landscapes of Sylvia Plath's poetry by well over a decade:

> Each night the dragnets of the tide
> take the shattered moon
> beyond the harbour bar
> but she reluctant suicide
> nibbles her freedom and returns
> to climb beside the nearest star.
> One clear night endures her pain
> to plunge to baptism again.

In her songs and ballads, sonnets and longer poems, as well as in her one-act play *The Uninvited*, MacCarthy shows real artistic ambition, matched by an at times unsettling disorientation, as in 'Old Toys':

> Breathe quietly now, the dolls are asleep.
> Old deaf and blind
> and sleep is kind ...
> ...
> the room grows chill,
> mouth open, jaw relaxed, they give
> the simulacrum of disordered death.
> Stiff effigies ...

In her varied translations it is interesting to note the early response (1935) to the Jewish poet Else Lasker-Schüler, who fled Nazi Germany in 1934, since another Trinity College graduate – the contemporary poet Eavan Boland – also translated Lasker-Schüler's poetry seventy years later, in *After Every War: Twentieth-Century Women Poets*. Also significant are MacCarthy's translations, which include 'Nächtliches Bild', one of Hans Bethge's poems, based upon Chinese verse, versions of which Gustav Mahler set to music in 'Das Lied von der Erde' ('The Song of the Earth').

This web of allusion, intertext and connection between various European artists across different languages underlines the cultural awareness MacCarthy shared with her Irish contemporaries. It all points to the fascinating strands of literary modernism with which she identified, alongside the more traditional forms of lullaby and song she took from the Spanish tradition, such as her reading of *The Oxford Book of Spanish Verse*, an exceptionally rich and intriguing body of work, which now comes into critical view. Several decades after she first published her translations and poems in significant outlets of the thirties and forties, including *Hermathena* (the long-established literary journal from Trinity College Dublin), the *Dublin Magazine* and

The Irish Times, her poems were broadcast by the Irish national broadcaster, Radio Éireann (originally known as RN2), and also included in the London-based *Sunday Referee* newspaper (home to some of Dylan Thomas's early poems). Three poems – 'Viaticum', 'Insomnia' and 'Ghosts' – were chosen for inclusion in an important, indeed groundbreaking anthology, *New Irish Poets*, edited by Devin A. Garrity and published in 1948 by Devin-Adair in the United States.

In the present edition of her poems, such promise and ambition is extended by the inclusion of *The Uninvited*, MacCarthy's poetic verse play. It all suggests just how much more there might have been for her to contribute had illness not cruelly struck her down at such a relatively early age. The tragedy – for her husband of barely three years, Con Leventhal, and her wider group of family and friends – is etched most starkly in the cluster of letters Samuel Beckett wrote on learning from Leventhal about the seriousness of her illness.

According to Knowlson, in November 1958 Beckett received a request from MacCarthy for him to visit her in Dublin 'for one last time'. He spent the first week of December travelling a number of times from The Shottery in Killiney to her and Leventhal's flat at 36 Lower Baggot Street. 'She seemed to have lost a lot of weight,' writes Knowlson,

> and as Beckett looked into her tired, drawn eyes, he remembered what he had written of their great beauty only a matter of months before. [*Krapp's Last Tape.*] Now, Ethna sat for most of the day crouching, silent, over the fire. He tried desperately hard to remain cheerful and positive for her and for Con's sake, encouraging her to go to London to see a Harley Street specialist. Yet all three knew that the end could not be long in coming and, on his last visit, he walked away choked with sorrow. [*Damned to Fame*] (pp. 459–60)

Beckett's distraught letter to her is its own kind of elegy for the woman he loved and greatly respected:

> Though we said little in Dublin I think all was said there and nothing to add for the moment. My silly old body is here alone with the snow and the crows and the exercise-book that opens like a door and lets me far down into the now friendly dark. I don't think, dear Ethna, I can be of any use just now, either to you or Con. But if you want me all you have to do is send for me. I send you again all that was always and will always be in my heart for you.
>
> [Texas University, Leventhal Collection, 1.7.
> *Letters*, Vol. 3, p. 195]

These letters to MacCarthy, deposited in the University of Texas, and also those to Con Leventhal, make for difficult reading as Beckett laments his helplessness in the face of her terminal illness. See, for instance, his letters to MacCarthy dated 4.2.59, 24.3.59 and those that mention her final days and his great sense of loss at her death in letters to family, friends and correspondents, including Molly Roe (6.2.59), Avigdor Arikha (12.3.59), Aidan Higgins (24.3.59), Barbara Bray (27.5.59) and Lawrence Harvey (3.10.60) where he requests that reference to a car crash involving Beckett as driver, causing Ethna to be hospitalized in the early thirties, should be removed from the text of an interview. 'Over thirty years later, [writes Knowlson] he confessed to Lawrence Harvey that he would "never forget the look in [Ethna's] father's eye afterwards" and the episode remained a nightmare that he could still not bear to talk about' (p. 143). Knowlson also makes the telling point that, on learning that MacCarthy was no longer to receive treatment for her condition except for painkilling injections, Beckett wrote to Con, 'Your letter leaves me in speechless sorrow' while continuing to write to MacCarthy, sending her magazines such as *Paris Match*.

'In March, he even picked a few tiny flowers in the wood near his Ussy house and sent them to her with the words: "This is just my heart to you and my hand in yours and a few wood violets I'd take from their haunt for no one else."' (Knowlson, *Damned to Fame*, p. 463)

Gerald Dawe

II

My association [writes Eoin O'Brien], if I may call it such, with Ethna MacCarthy began in the 1960s when I became fascinated by Samuel Beckett's *More Pricks than Kicks*. At that time I was working as a house physician to Alan Thompson in the Richmond Hospital. Oddly, I did not know of his close association with the Beckett family dating back to their schoolboy days at Portora, although the framed passport photograph hanging in his office should have alerted me to the friendship. Con Leventhal, with whom I would become friendly later, married Ethna MacCarthy in 1956. I suspect that she found the irascible charm and humour of this erudite Dubliner irresistible and his sheer irreverence must have found a like heart in a woman with daring propensities, given the restrictive mores of the period:

> We are the offspring of a gin and vermouth in a local public-house. We swore that we were young and could assert our youth with all its follies. We railed against the psychopedantic parlours of our elders and their maidenly consorts, hoping the while with an excess of Picabia and banter, a whiff of Dadaist Europe to kick Ireland into artistic wakefulness.
> [L.K.E. (A.J. Leventhal), 'Confessional', *The Klaxon*, Winter 1923–4, p. 1]

I cannot remember precisely how I met Con Leventhal in Paris but what I do recall is that we became instant friends. Con lived on Boulevard Montparnasse with his partner, Marion Leigh, and whenever I visited Paris (often with my wife, Tona) we joined them for drinks under the watchful eye of Cecil Salkeld's frame-flowing portrait of Con, before crossing the boulevard to La Coupole for dinner. And when Con and Marion came to Dublin, we would dine at our house on Clifton Terrace in Monkstown where long literary discussions would go on into the night. Sometimes we were joined by other friends, among whom I remember the artist William Hayter, discussing intently with Tona the idiosyncrasies of colour perception, which he demonstrated with vibrant gesture in the overmantel mirror.

During one of my visits to Paris, I confided to Con that a project I had embarked upon was giving me a new appreciation of Beckett's writings – namely that the importance of Irish (mostly Dublin) place, character, humour and nuance was being missed by the many writers (most of whom were not Irish) in the then growing volume of secondary literature. I showed him how, in my cycling peregrinations of the city, the mountains and the coast, I identified place, and sometimes person, in the novels, drama and poetry and that this was making me acutely aware of the 'reality of the unreal', in support of what Con had once called the 'unreality of the real'. I think Con saw that, through the medium of photography, I was giving a visual perspective to what he had expressed with conviction in words. Indeed, I did not know then that he had once made the plaintive plea: 'In parenthesis and a new paragraph may I ask when we are going to have an illustrator of B's work?' Although at this time I met Con frequently in Paris, and although we often discussed Beckett's work, I had never presumed to ask to meet Beckett. That is until, one day, Con said to me that he had spoken with Beckett about my excursions into the landscape of his writing and that he had expressed a willingness to meet me. But that is another story, one that led to a wonderful friendship, out of which arose *The Beckett Country: Samuel Beckett's Ireland.*

*

On his last visit to Dublin in 1979, it was sadly clear that Con was dying from cancer and I accompanied him and Marion back to Montparnasse to give him what little solace I could. He died shortly afterwards, and I missed greatly his mischievous Jewish humour and our talks on life and literature. Much as I may have missed him, it was nothing to the loss Beckett felt. He had lost not only his close friend, but also his trusted and learned confidant who also protected him from the frivolous multitude clamouring at his door.

I determined to do something to honour this remarkable man of letters, who had been the first to praise *Ulysses*, who had written a criticism of Dublin theatre from the thirties to the fifties, and who had been a formidable influence on one of the century's greatest writers. I brought together a group of Con's friends to consider how best to commemorate his erudition, charm and literary influence. We agreed to establish a scholarship that would enable a graduate student in English or Modern Languages of Trinity College Dublin to study in Europe.

Con's literary associates, and academic institutions at home and abroad, contributed generously to the scholarship fund and to the scholarship auction, which was held in the Samuel Beckett Rooms in Trinity College on 15 March 1984. The funds raised from this event have enabled over thirty postgraduate recipients of the Leventhal Scholarship to travel to various parts of the world to pursue their studies.

Shortly after Con's death, on one of my visits to Marion in the flat on Montparnasse, she gave me a case of papers, diaries and notebooks with the admonition 'you will know what to do with these'. Among this trove of literary gems was a notebook containing the poems written by Con's deceased wife, Ethna MacCarthy, some typed, some in handwriting and some inserted from publications. About ten years ago I typed these remarkable poems with a view to assembling a collection of her poetry, but I abandoned the notion until recently, when I showed them to Gerald Dawe, who immediately rekindled my enthusiasm, and we decided to publish the poems.

Leaving critical commentary on the poetic talents of this multifaceted woman to Gerald, I would like to comment on the likely influences medicine may have had on her poetry. Ethna MacCarthy, as we have seen, was subject to both medical and poetic inspirations in childhood. It was common then (and still is, though to a lesser extent) for the sons and daughters of a doctor to be persuaded in their choice of career by parental influences. However, it appears that MacCarthy's initial tendencies were towards literary study, but in the mid-1930s she diverted to enter the TCD School of Medicine, graduating in 1941 with a degree in medicine and surgery, and in 1946 she was awarded a postgraduate doctorate. Her medical interest was health in children, and she was appointed physician to the children's dispensary at the Royal City of Dublin Hospital. She left this post in 1954, hopeful of being appointed to the World Health Organization, but failed the obligatory physical examination.

Her contributions to the *Irish Journal of Medical Science* on topics relating to public health problems in childhood were few. However modest her scientific contributions may be, the influence of medicine on her poetry is often very deliberate, whereas at other times medical allusions are subtle, perhaps unconscious references, simply deriving from a familiarity with the language of clinical practice. Take, as example, the profoundly philosophical utterance 'All things stiffen from this same disease / we only, die of being born.' ('Advent') or 'endless aspergillum play to lay this cold and lovely dust' ('Ghosts'). Or again the references to 'ephemeridae' and 'the Brownian motes' ('Shutters') are concepts arising most likely from instruction in the subjects of botany and physiology in her early medical curriculum. In the poetic drama 'The Uninvited' there are prescient references to the influence of genetic science on human behaviour.

But it is the poetry dealing unashamedly with the practice of medicine that is of most interest, because in these MacCarthy imparts to the life of her time a deep acceptance of what existence is, without necessarily anticipating change, or perhaps surprisingly, without voicing criticism of the poverty and its inevitable companion, misery. This philosophical acceptance of life as it pertains to her existence as a doctor is not far removed from Beckett's 'You must go on. I can't go on. I'll go on' acceptance of the human condition. There is another interpretation of this apparent passivity, and that is that the poetry of Ethna MacCarthy viewed through the lens of time allows us to reassess social and medical progress nearly a century on.

Her success of graduating as a doctor was a moment of poetic questioning, a crossroad of doubt expressed in 'MB, BCh, BAO' (originally entitled 'Farewell') in which she ponders with fear the new life ahead:

> Ferreted from a five-year cave,
> expelled from this earthy womb confused,
> my eyes assaulted by the light,
> I am at bay in feeble fear.

Turning to the poetry depicting medical life and practice, she expresses in 'The Theatre' the fears of the trainee doctor, who, then as now, having worked long hours and deprived of sleep, fears the lack of concentration: 'Sweat and heat – I must not fall / on my drowsy feet.'

> The clock on the wall
> has surely stopped still
> Sister is watching me – some mistake?
> I must keep awake, I must keep awake.

The subservience of the anaesthetist to the surgeon is depicted with humour: '"How is the new patient?" the surgeon barks / "Still here" the anaesthetist remarks . . .' In 'Viaticum', the omnipotent night nurse is given a presence often taken for granted:

> The nurses chart its course all night
> and those who drowse and those who tell their beads
> and those who coma vigil keep.

In 'Clinic', the observing eye of the poet portrays the sadness of a sick young girl, a sight so often seen but rarely given presence; the poem culminates in this sad waif's elevation to dignity in life's panoply of drudgery and misfortune:

> Disowned by father, dispossessed
> of childhood's dynasty,
> her foster mother's love disdained,
> in dignity she walks a world defiled;
> like bitter aloes in her lovely mouth
> the arid lonely words – nurse-child.

MacCarthy's interest in medicine was the effect of poverty on childhood health and this is reflected forcibly in 'Nell Gwynn', in which the filth of deprivation and the inevitable accompaniment of infestation is shockingly portrayed:

On Saturday the maggots sprout their wings,
and glamorous Dublin clad in shoddy silk
conceals her sores with regal air
ecstatic lice rejoice in carefully curled and uncombed hair.
And after all what harm?
Dublin is still the courtesan of Kings,
the wit, the laughing eyes are there
but what if dirt has lost its charm?

Two poems are dedicated solely to the practice of medicine in Dublin: 'The Charity', a commemorative ode written to celebrate the bicentenary celebrations of the Rotunda Hospital, Dublin's oldest maternity hospital, and 'Vale', a tribute to her teacher and mentor in Baggot Street Hospital, Alfred R. Parsons. The theme of 'The Charity' is a tribute to Bartholomew Mosse, a Georgian obstetrician who devoted his life and money to founding a 'lying-in hospital' for the poor pregnant women of Dublin who, in the Georgian era, were without any institutional care:

This is Dublin, till one valiant heart
moved by this misery and piteous loss
made himself champion of their part
soldier and surgeon, Bartholomew Mosse
with hands and brain and scanty purse, alone
transformed a vision into stone
and lit it with a purpose that has shone
across two hundred years [.]

MacCarthy's tribute to Alfred Parsons, 'Vale' is, I believe, unique in being the only genuine poetic tribute to a practising physician (if we leave aside Swift's somewhat ambiguous witticisms to his physician Richard Helsham). In this poem MacCarthy not only pays tribute to an exceptional clinician who used the then popular form of bedside teaching to illustrate illness in a patient to an assembly of students who would have travelled from the medical schools of the city to Baggot Street Hospital, but she also captures 'Alfie's' innate kindness and his understanding of student sensitivities:

> How praise this ardent life
> this straight devotion, this learned anchorite
> who taught the children
> nursery rhymes?
> Physician, chemist who had time
> to see a troubled student's private pain,
> scarce pausing his brisk thread
> to leave his wisdom
> in the anguished brain
> as follies for a foolish heart,
> unheard by all his glittering train
> of student satellites.

In that time streptococcal infection was common and those afflicted often went on to develop disease of the valves of the heart (rheumatic fever), which was manifest in a variety of murmurs, audible with a stethoscope. To have any hope of passing the final clinical examination, students had to become adept at diagnosing these cardiac abnormalities. Parsons was renowned for his ability to not only diagnose the murmurs, but also to convey this skill to students. The poem closes with a poignant lament for the passing of a beloved teacher and clinician:

> Ever alert of step, and ear and eye
> we had forgotten he could die
> and when he did, so live was he
> confused, we wondered why.

His was the green old age of the god
that sadly watched a world decay.
Now the dark ferry paddles him away,
but as black Charon dips his blade
the god will say
'He is the immortal
I the shade.'

Eoin O'Brien

III

In preparing this selection of Ethna MacCarthy's poems for publication, we have simply placed the poems according to their date of writing. With some of the unpublished poems we have had to make our own judgement as to their date of writing by reference to their chronological appearance in her notebook. It should be emphasized that *Poems* is an interim publication based largely upon material discovered in an archive bequeathed to Eoin O'Brien and now deposited at the Library of Trinity College Dublin.

We would like to acknowledge the generous assistance and encouragement of the Woolfson family for this book. At Trinity College Dublin the invaluable financial support of the Trinity College Dublin Association and Trust, Professor Michael Gill and the School of Medicine, Sinéad Pentony, Associate Director, Trinity Development and Alumni, Dr Conor Linnie for his research assistance, Dr Julie Bates for her advice, the eagle-eyed Jonathan Williams, Dr Jane Maxwell, Trinity College Library, the photographer Stephen Whitehorne and all at The Lilliput Press.

It is our hope that the editing of this collection of poems will provide the impetus for a fully fledged biographical and literary study of Ethna MacCarthy and her contemporaries, based on the archival material related to her life and work to be found in Trinity College Dublin, along with the archives of Con Leventhal, Denis Johnston and Samuel Beckett. As one can see here, Ethna MacCarthy's publication record follows a fairly typical pattern of progression from university magazine (*Hermathena*) to local literary journal (*Dublin Magazine*) to national newspaper (*The Irish Times*) and broadcaster (RN2/RTÉ) and international platforms such as the somewhat quixotic *Sunday Referee* and the important, era-defining anthology *New Irish Poets*. Had an individual volume of her poems beckoned in the 1950s, she certainly would have had the necessary record of publication and significant peer endorsements. While this was not to be, our posthumous edition is intended as the reclamation of her missing poetic voice and is dedicated to Ethna MacCarthy's memory; a very special, multitalented and humane Irish woman.

Eoin O'Brien & Gerald Dawe

POEMS

The Virgin's Lullaby

Flying in the palm trees
Angels watch you keep
Still all the branches that my Child
may sleep.

Bethlehem palms
stirred by a breeze,
when fierce winds sweep
loud toss the trees.
Hush! winds, creep.
Quiet please.
Still all the branches that my Child
may sleep.

The Holy Child
has need of rest.
Earth made Him weep,
now peace is best.
Silence deep on
tears blest.
Still all the branches that my Child
may sleep.

Icicles chill
gather close by
Snow drifts heap
No shelter nigh
Angels keep

watch on high
*Still all the branches that my Child
may sleep.*

['Cantâreillo de la Vírgin' by
Lope de Vega Carpio (1562–
1635). From *The Oxford Book of
Spanish Verse*, 6 May 1935. *The
Dublin Magazine*, Vol. X, No.
4, p. 13, October–December
1935.]

Dublin Castle

The dead are buried
and the blossom is out.
Stertor of pencils snoring lines,
where the heat haze binds the turret tops
and sea gulls cry like snakes.
Tick-tack-time!
A shower of almond blossom
on the radiant dead:
and silent silt of dust
singing on parched window panes.
Five sharp! the workers gone
like snow flakes on the bosom of the water.
Slow squats the swollen sun on city spires,
and in the lilac-hued exhausted air
the white cat moults,
and Spring is born
in Winter's slough.

[Archive poem, 27 May 1935.]

World's End

The world is full of weeping
as if God Himself were dead:
heavier than burial clay
the leaden shadows spread.
Come! Let us lie yet closer hid.
In every heart the life-urge sleeps
underneath a coffin lid.
Kiss me again and closer lie!
For pulsing longing ever leaps
to that same world where we must die.

[Rendering of 'Weltende' by Else Lasker-Schüler, from the German, 10 June 1935.]

The Prisoner's Song

The month was of May
and in the heat
when nightingales
and larks compete
and lovers
lovers' vows repeat
I alone unhappy
prisoner in a cell
daytime from the night
cannot tell
listening for a little bird
that sang the dawn to greet.
One day an archer shot him.
God grant he may with evil meet!

[Unpublished version, 22 October
1935.]

The Prisoner's Song

The month was of May
and in the heat
the lark was singing
— the nightingales sweet
when lovers
lovers' vows repeat.
I alone, unhappy
in my prison cell
if it is the day or night
cannot tell
only for a little bird
that always sang the dawn to greet.
One day an archer shot him.
God grant he may with evil meet.

[A version of the fifteenth-century
romance 'El Prisonero', *Hermathena*,
No. 64, November 1944, p. 141.]

Das ist mein Streit

This is my strait
visionary dedicate,
to breast the days' monotony
then intimate,
to grasp life's myriad mystery
of earthily ganglia writhing free:
and then my suffering ecstasy translate
beyond Life's history,
and Time's estate.

[From the German of Rainer Maria
Rilke for the *Sunday Referee*, 7 July 1935.
Published in *The Dublin Magazine*, Vol.
XVI, No. 1, p. 8, January–March 1941.]

Nächtliches Bild

I

Under the flail if the wind flies the white chaff of the pond
Then the waters grow still, tranquilly brimming from rim to rim.
The fishes leap, their gleaming scales
Like dusky lotus flowering in the night.
In the path of the swimming moon
Tree and cloud clear-etched Night's silver disc
Transmutes the dew to fiery pearls
That shimmer through the magic night.

[A rendering into English of 'Nächtliches Bild' by Hans Bethge
after the Chinese, 7 August 1935.]

II

The wind slaps the white caps of the pond
Then quieted the listless water lies
And fishes rise white-bellied
As the bursting lotus flower at night.
And tree and cloud stand stark
Before the reeling moon.
Night's alchemistic silver disc coagulates
The fragile dew to fatted pearls
That feed their splendour
Through the dazzled night.

[A further rendering of Bethge's poem, published in *The Dublin
Magazine*, Vol. XVI, No. 1, p. 9, January–March 1941.]

Tomorrow

Tomorrow's radiant face is veiled,
only her eyes
wide open gaze
in mild surmise
at all the yesterdays.
Silent they follow her high destiny
through colourful bazaar and narrow street.
Serene she walks on tiny feet
through all the throng and stench
and quivering heat:
until she sighs,
'How strange and devious is the way
to Paradise.'

[Archive poem, 8 July 1935.]

Wir schreiten auf ...

Under the beech trees we patrolled
up and down as far as the gate
and from the alleyway's glinting gold
saw the trellised almond blossoming late.

And sought the benches unhaunted by shade
where no strange voice could our ears affright
in dreams our palsied arms are stayed
and we are laved in gentle light.

Our mood is gracious as the murmurous drone
and dappled radiance from the high tree tops.
Hearing and heeding nothing, save alone
the thud of ripe fruit as it drops.

['Wir schreiten auf ...' by Stefan George for the
Sunday Referee. Second prize of 10s. 6d., 20 October
1935. Later published in *Hermathena*, Vol. 26, No.
51, May 1938, p. 153.]

Cossante

See yonder tree with leaves sunlit
something surely pleases it.

That tree so lovely to behold
will soon its tender buds unfold.

Something, something pleases it.
Yonder tree so fair to see

wants to blossom gloriously
something must have pleased it.

Already the tender buds unfold:
lo! Behold.

Now the blossom is bursting free
Come and see!

Look! Something pleased it
certainly

women are gathering the fruit of the tree.
Something, something pleased it!

[Diego Hurtado de Mendoza, 1904, 27
October 1935. Christmas card, 1940, *Farmer's
Gazette*, 13 February 1943.]

Sonnet

These things that were all wonder and delight
awakened at the dawn's first morning glow,
by evening will be piteously laid low
falling asleep in the cold arms of night.
This hue that challenges the sky's birthright,
this rainbow woven scarlet gold and snow
serves as a warning of all mortal woe:
striving to span the world while there is light.
The roses early bourgeon into bloom,
that they may sooner wither in their bowers:
finding the bud their cradle and their tomb.
Thus men may read their fortune in the flowers:
whose very day of birth is day of doom;
for bygone centuries are made of hours.

[Calderón de la Barca (1600–1681). Sonnet spoken
by Don Fernando in the second act of *El Príncipe
Constante*, 6 May 1940. Sonnet (from the Spanish
of Calderón) beginning 'These things that were
all wonder and delight', *The Dublin Magazine*, Vol.
X, No. 4, p. 12, October–December 1935.]

Sonatina

The Princess is sad — what can ail the Princess
whose rose-lipped mouth utters sighs of distress?
Her laughter is stilled and her colour is flown,
pale is the Princess on her golden throne,
the keys of the spinet are mute, and alone
in a vase forgot swoons a flower full-blown.

In the royal gardens peacocks preen their wings,
the old Duenna chatters foolish things,
a scarlet jester pirouettes and mimes
the Princess does not laugh, the Princess does not listen
but watches the wings of a dragon-fly glisten,
bearing a dream to faery climes.

Thinks she of Golconda's Prince or the Chinese one?
Or him who unharnessed his chariot in the sun
that his eyes might compass the softness of the light?
Is she thinking of the King of the rose-attared isles,
Or is it the Sovereign of the diamonds that beguiles
Or Ormuzd's proud master of the pearls of delight?

Poor little Princess of the rose-lipped mouth
who longs to be a butterfly — a swallow going South,
to fly through the sky on airy wings — be free!
to climb the sun's ladder on a luminous ray,
to salute all the lilies with the lyrics of May
or merge in the wind above the thunder of the sea.

She heeds not the palace, the silver distaff for the wool,
the balcony enchanted, the scarlet capering fool,
or the swans in the azure lake sailing abreast.
The flowers of the court, their sadness breathe forth.
Jasmine from the Orient, lilies from the north,
the petals of the Southern rose and dahlias from the west.

Poor little Princess of the azure eyes
caught by your golden chains, held by silken ties,
the royal Palace is a marble cage
proudly protected by its guards from all alarms
by the hundred halberds of its negro men-at-arms,
a sleepless greyhound and a mighty dragon's rage.

'Would I were a chrysalis bursting free my bonds!'
(The Princess is pale. The Princess desponds.)
'O roseate vision in gold and ivory drawn,
would that I could fly to some Prince of fairy tale!'
(The Princess is sad. The Princess is pale.)
'Who was lovelier than April and brighter than the dawn!'

'Hush!' the fairy godmother of a sudden cried,
'On a horse with wings I see him ride
with his sword on his hip and his hawk on glove
the knight from afar who has conquered death,
who loves you and longs with every breath
to set fire to your lips with the kiss of love!'

[Rubén Darío (1867–1916), 10 January 1937. *Hermathena*,
November 1940.]

Eheu!

Here by this Latin Sea
The truth appears.
In rocks and olive tree and wine
I feel my years.

Oh God how old I am!
How old! You only know.
Whence comes my song
– And I? Whither do I go?

Learning to know myself,
The substance that is I
Costs me so much despair
– The 'how' – the 'why'.

What use this satin light
This dazzling sky
At the opening to the pit
Of the 'I', or the 'non-I'.

Whispers I had meant
To understand
Confided by the wind
The sea, the land.

Of being or not being
And such doubts clarify
– fragments of conscience.

Today — and days gone by

As this in a desert
Then I cried out my fears
But the sun was a corpse —
— I burst into tears.

[Rubén Darío, March 1937. *Herma-thena*, Vol. 26, No. 51, May 1938.]

Ballad of Julianesa

Up hounds and out! Plague take the dogs!
On Fridays eating meat, on Thursdays killing hogs.
Seven years I roam these vales
with unshod feet and bleeding nails
raw bones my food, my drink red blood of slaughter
seeking Julianesa the Emperor's own daughter
whom the Moors stole one early dawn
on the morning of St Juan
where in her father's orchard she
gathered roses happily.
Julianesa heard him, wrapt in the Moor's embrace
the tears sprang from her eyes
and smote her captor's face.

[Translation of 'Romance de Julianese', 6 April 1937.
Hermathena, No. 56, November 1940.]

Ballad of Count Arnaldos

Who has ever had such fortune
on all the waters of the sea,
as befell the Count Arnaldos
on the morning of St John!
With his falcon poised on his wrist,
out at the chase a hunting he,
saw a galleon sailing in,
careening under shrouds of silk
her fragile rigging spun like gauze.
The mariner commanding her
coming to harbour sang a song
that soothed and becalmed the sea,
and lulled the fretful winds to sleep
and made the fishes in the depths
rise to the surface of the bay,
and wheeling birds about the mast
came from the air and settled down.
Whereon the Count Arnaldos spoke,
heed well the words he made to say:
'In God's name tell me mariner,
this song of yours what may it be?'
The mariner replied to him:
this is the answer that he gave:
'I'll sing this song alone for him
who comes and sails the seas with me.'

[Archive poem.]

Ballad of St Simon's

In Seville there is a monastery,
it is St Simon's so they say,
whither all the high born ladies
make their pilgrimage to pray.
And there my lovely lady goes,
beauteous 'mid beauty without stint.
In gown on gown she graceful flows.
The sunflower in her mantle dreams,
her pretty mouth so like a rose
of scarlet salve just bears a hint
the pallor of that face's snows
is heightened by a carmine tint,
beneath those eye-lids tinged with Kohl
the shadowed azure brighter seems.
Standing in the chapel door
as radiant as the sun she gleams.
Lo! the good priest at the altar
stops in the mass he celebrates
the acolytes dumbfounded falter
each in responses hesitates.
Who piped 'Amen! Amen!' before
now sighs confused 'amor! amor!'

[Christmas card, 1939.]

Ballad of the Washer Girl

Mother, the sun had just risen
On the morning of St John,
When I saw along the sea shore
A damozel all unaware.
Alone she washed, alone she wrung,
Alone spread on a rose-bush tree
The drying linen, meanwhile she
Went singing this song to the air:
'Where is my love, Oh where is he?
To seek him whither shall I fare?'
And wandering up and down the sea
She went thus singing in despair.
A golden comb was in her hand
With which she made to comb her hair.
'Good mariner,' she said to me.
'As God keeps you from all harm free,
Tell me if you have seen my love,
Pray have you seen him anywhere?'

[Archive poem.]

Ballad of the Wedding in France

A wedding feast there was in France,
the heart of Paris was its scene.
And who of all would lead the dance
but Beatrice the revel's Queen!
And who on her should fix his glance
of all that throng but Don Martin!
'Good Count, good Count, I beg you say
what is it makes your gaze so keen?
Are you just looking at the dance,
or is it me you look at pray?'
'I am not looking at the dance,
for many dances I have seen.
It is your beauty's wond'rous sway
that does my mortal eyes entrance.'
'Good Count, then let us run away,
if that is what you really mean.
My husband is too old and grey
to overtake our dalliance.
to follow us and our romance.'

[Archive poem.]

Exile

Beloved, my life has ebbed again
To a child's estate uncertain, chill,
Wan as November's willows suppliant wreathed.
Once more with tender love confirm
My wraithlike womanhood,
And comfort me with stately names,
Egyptian princess, flower, and give
Chrism for my eyes and ears,
But no salt for my mouth:
Unarmed and childlike would I seek
Such sanctuary.

[*The Irish Times*, Saturday, 28 September 1940.]

Renewal

The seething cauldron boils and heat
scourges the maddened particles' blind race
into a chaos of collision,
that churning flicks the empty bubbles into space
and in this fevered frenzied vision
'Faster! faster!' the speed-mad white Queen screams,
as down the wind her crazed hair snaps and streams,
and lower sinks the curdled brew;
for heat and speed are twins
and none can tell apart these sibling two.
The brindled serpent now uncoils his might –
father of men who still his stigma hear –
patched in his horrid atavistic heat.
But when the flames are drowned in jungle night,
dark silent men from India will come
to tread the embers with their naked feet,
and charm the serpent to his sluggish lair.
And after another aeon pass
when summer rain lies soft upon the grass,
a simple sandaled friar will bless
with calm, this new untutored wilderness
matrixed in human blood and human tears,
like that old monk who heard a nightingale
and stood entranced three hundred years.

[January 1941. Broadcast 20 January, 2RN.]

Spring Song

Spring has returned again:
Sound the pipes and give the dancers scope
Spreading wide upon the plain
Her green mantle – hope.

The breeze blows warm and soft:
Sound the pipes and give the dancers scope.
Clouds scudding swift aloft
Disclose the azure skies of hope.

The flower laughs hooded in the bud:
Sound the pipes and gives the dancers scope.
Rippling sings the waters' flood
The hallowed power of hope.

Hear you that trill that fills the air?
Sound the pipes and give the dancers scope
Open – for the swallow is there
Returning on the wings of hope.

Maiden, modest maiden:
Sound the pipes and give the dancers scope
May with merriment is laden
Whose coming bears your secret hope.

Love lies over all the land:
Sound the pipes and give the dancers scope
And in every heart is fanned

The germinating fragrance — hope.

Humming where the fresh green shows:
Sound the pipes and give the dancers scope
And as the drone and verdure grows
So too rises hope.

Songs, colour, scent:
Sound the pipes and give the dancers scope
Now in hymns of love are blent
Merging into hymns of hope.

Springtime in its turn will die:
Sound the pipes and give the dancers scope
But every year the meadows lie
Mantled once again — in hope.

Life's young innocence alone:
Silence the pipes and let the dancers mope
Alas! returns again to none
Mine is lost, and with it — hope.

[Don Pablo Piferrer (1818–1848), *Las Cien
Mejores Poesias*, p. 377, 18 July 1941.]

The Invitation

'Mariana a toast I bring
on Sunday wedding bells will ring.'
'That wedding should be mine,
Don Alonso – not another's.'
'But I am not the bridegroom
the wedding is my brother's.'
'Pray be seated Don Alonso,
on this flowered settle rest,
that to my future husband
my father did bequest.'
Down he sat and soon,
Don Alonso slept.
Then Mariana stealthily
into her flowery garden crept.
Sublimate of mercury
blood of vipers three
a live lizard's skin
bone of a toad's shin
and ounces four
of steel ground fine.
These did she pour
into the wine
'Drink, Don Alonso
wine with me.'
'First you Mariana
as custom wills.'
Then Mariana stealthily
the wine into her bosom spills.

Don Alonso manlike
drinks it at a draught,
all his teeth are drawn
by the venom he has quaffed.
'What's in the wine Mariana
the wine you gave to me?'
'Sublimate of mercury
blood of vipers three,
a live lizard's skin
bone of a toad's shin
and ounces four
of steel ground fine.'
'Cure me, cure me I implore
that wed you may be mine.'
'Don Alonso you cry in vain
already your heart is split in twain.'
'Bride of my soul goodbye
so soon your widowhood will be begun.
Good-bye beloved parents
so soon to be without a son.
On a piebald horse
I left my home
in a box of pine
to the Church I come.'

[*Le Strango Collection*, 29 July 1941. *The Dublin Magazine*, Vol. XVII, No. 1, pp. 13–14, January–March 1942.]

MB, BCh, BAO

Ferreted from a five-year cave,
expelled from this earthy womb confused,
my eyes assaulted by the light,
I am at bay in feeble fear.
And over my closed transparent lids
there swings the blood red curtain of the sun
that hunted creature must know well in frost,
cowering in lust for sleep,
lulled by the hunters' steady step
that crushes the crepitating snow.
Will this red shutter ever rise on my torpidity
and let my eyes see the bog cotton waving wantonly
to the striding shadows of the others gone.

[Archive poem, original title 'Farewell'. Probably writ-
ten in 1942 after graduation.]

Nell Gwynn

The patina of Dublin holds your image still,
the copper glint of unshawled hair bleached
by wind and rain, perfumed by flowers
and offal of back streets
and Andalusian cozening eyes beguile
and cheat, simply as a right, a trade
for stale food, stored under a bed unmade,
two oranges a penny Nell!
fish and violets and asphodel,
this is still your century and who cares
or ever learnt to care about the smell?
On Saturday the maggots sprout their wings,
and glamorous Dublin clad in shoddy silk
conceals her sores with regal air
ecstatic lice rejoice in carefully curled and uncombed hair.
And after all what harm?
Dublin is still the courtesan of Kings,
the wit, the laughing eyes are there
but what if dirt has lost its charm?

[Archive poem.]

The Shrine

My silver cat with burning eyes
thinks the wall a paradise
for angling human kind.
She knows the world belongs to her
for her to rend or kill or bless,
the very wind that stirs her fur
she tolerates as a caress
ruffling a can-can glimpse of white
beneath pale infant loveliness.
Intent she concentrates upon
the pilgrims' passers-by,
for careless they might miss the sign
of granite sparkling in the sun
that lights her wayside shrine
the Sphinx like the brindled paws
silica bright her agate uncurled claws
hoisted the feather tail unfurled.
Exquisite stretch and studied pink-tongued yawn;
thus the arch priestess greets her conquered world
worshippers pause in praise and prayer
into that subtle dove grey fur.
Each thinks he is the only one
soothed and solaced by a purr.
But what is this? Some infidel has brought
a filthy dog into this hallowed street.
Fury stiffens every hair
and fans it like a peacock's tail.
Panache becomes a twitching flail

and murder broods upon the air.
The stupid dog has scampered by
beneath that lambent amber eye
ignorant and unaware of it.
His master should have had the wit
to know that even the big green bus
has made this shrine a terminus.

[20 December 1941, *The Dublin Magazine*, Vol.
XVII, No. 2, p. 8, April–June 1942. Title by
Seamus O'Sullivan.]

The Skeleton Speaks

The trunks are old and filled with dust
that once was lust.
While prosy letters to be sure
are gravely scanned as literature
yet halfpenny stamps are treasure trove
that justify the cost of love
and wild words crystallised in print
now stilled in death are worth a mint,
old dreams and samples safe to handle
and these quiet bones reclothed in scandal.

[Archive poem, 23 December 1941.]

Medusa

Beauty like hers must never make
the same unnatural mistake
of showing itself to mortal eyes.
In her the last dread gorgon dies
wise lavish mother of a motley brood
she scents the litter for that fatal blood
and when she hears a silver kit
softly and gently murders it.

[Archive poem, 23 December 1941.]

The Blind Man's Faith

The holy Virgin travelled
on her way to Bethlehem.
A Child in her arms she carried;
a heavenly sight to see,
and as they followed the road,
to drink, the Child asked thirstily.
'Ask not for water, my treasure,
ask not, my baby, for see,
the rivers are running turbid,
the rivulets filled with mud.
None can drink of such water
and the fountains are weeping blood.'
High on the hill above
stood a sweet orange grove
bent with its golden burden,
it was laden so heavily.
A blindman was its guardian,
a blind man who could not see.
'Blind man, give me an orange,
for the Child give one to me.'
'Pluck the oranges, lady,
take as many as you like.
Gather the biggest among them
and leave the small to grow ripe.'
Where she gathered them one by one,
a hundred clustered anew on the stem,
bowing down the orange tree.
The blind man then began to see

and cried: 'Who can these strangers be
that such good fortune bring with them?'
It was the blessed Virgin
on the road to Bethlehem.

[From the *Le Strango Collection*, 6 August 1941.
Christmas card 1941 from Ethna MacCarthy,
'Desmond', Sandymount Avenue, Dublin.
The Farmer's Gazette, 2 June 1943.]

Viaticum

The sluice gates of sleep are open wide
And through the House its soothing silver tide
From ward to ward flows grave and deep;
Now flood, now fretful trickle,
And some it leaves marooned
Who cannot sleep.
The nurses chart its course all night
And those who drowse and those who tell their beads
And those who coma vigil keep.
Sunken beyond the lure of light –
Some watch the shadows with unfocused eyes,
Dull and indifferent, ears attuned
To soundless music of the Boatman's oar
And rhythmic singing of the rowlocks' strain
As the dark ferry swings to shore.
An old old woman and a little child
Soon will meet each other there
But who knows what gay roisterer
Before this dawn will pay their fare.

[*The Irish Times*, Saturday, 11 April 1942.]

The Theatre
(The probationer's song)

Green white enamel and sunlight and steel
And every gowned figure tense.
Only the patient cannot feel
Hush and ritual – ether incense
Sweat and heat – I must not fall
On my drowsy feet.
Ether is sweet – ether is sweet.
This won't do at all
I seem to sway
Holding this tray
Waiting and waiting
(What *did* sister say?)
The clock on the wall
Has surely stopped still
Sister is watching me – some mistake?
I must keep awake I must keep awake
Two pigeons stare from the window sill
Nudging each other's wings –
Sometimes they say the strangest things ...
And the fever bright eyes criticise
Thanks to Sister and surgeon too
Though all they do is coo-coo
'Nurse' (that is Sister's subdued abuse
I know, she knows I'm not much use)
My God I nearly dropped this tray
'How is the new patient?' the surgeons barks
'Still here' the anaesthetist remarks

At last he's taking off the cover
And I can go
This operation's over.

[Archive poem, 6 September 1942.]

Requiem

'Rest,' to me the wise ones croon,
but rest like shadow needs an ardent noon
and in disuse its pallid embers fall,
as papery scabious wilts in senile warmth
beneath September's purpling wall.
Give back the rebel summer days
with their short deep repose.
Oh! stay the chill chrysanthemum,
and give me back the flagrant rose.
Turn fast the sanded hoop of hours
or let my rest lie buried under flowers.

[*The Irish Times*, 10 October 1942.]

Harlequin

My love is of the moon
pale sequin and velvet cratered depths,
pure light and softest shaggy dark.
Like her he seeks the sun for warmth
to ramble the livid streets from dusk
and barter his tranquillity for tears,
and never knows how good he is
or tired, but fights the sordid strident day
till like a child he rests a little in my arms.
And then the fearful maturation of the light
lifts at his languid head. And so he goes,
to skim the scattered sequins from the pools.

[*The Irish Times*, 10 October 1942.]

War and the Rose

I sometimes think that never blows so red
The Rose as where some buried Caesar bled
               Omar Khayyam

From Caesar's blood the wild briar draws its life
and scarlet seeks a thousand years' revenge
its puffy circus offspring to avenge,
perfumed emasculate from the pruning knife,
fed on horse droppings, dropsical and then
left languish by a boudoir fire.
Oh! anguish of outcast gipsy briar
pinned and ragged on the wet hedgerows.
But now black bombs are bursting like a rose
and dropping make manure of men.
The gardener will fulfil his trust;
by his dead side the rabid knife is rust.
And all the roses will grow red again.

[*The Irish Times*, Saturday, 2 January 1943.]

Advent

Gay geisha of the spring the almond blossom flaunts
her fragile finery
beneath the darkening eye of March,
ignores the taunts
of winter's tottering mockery
nor heeds the screaming seagulls dip and pass
flashing their storm stained shadows on the glass
of shops in Grafton Street,
but crisp and neat
awaits a foreign festival:
while down the chill canal
bright brittle surfaces reflect
dark tousled trees
who genuflect
jostled by a hurrying breeze.
Within in the nests
the immortal egg unshattered rests.
And dying eyes grown puzzled and forlorn
reproach our grief with gentle alien scorn
saying: 'All things stiffen from this same disease;
we only die of being born.'

[*The Irish Times,* Easter Saturday, 24 April 1943.]

Ghosts

A ripple of dust, panicked across
a busy street
timidly darting through horses' feet
and I saw a well beloved ghost,
walk haltingly up
to the Provost's house.
But I was not near
and in a daze
watched the dust dwindle and disappear
and the light grow bleak
from the muffled skies
battening down hope
on my famished eyes.
What do they seek
so patiently?
Have we broken trust
that they turn away
and never speak.
Or must
our parched eyes
endless aspergillum play
to lay this cold and lovely dust?

[*The Dublin Magazine*, Vol. XVIII, No. 4,
pp. 67–8, October–December 1943.]

Barcelona

Being ill I ate
only hake and white grapes
in the land of wine,
and the mariners talked
of ships and iodine.
Cockroaches crawled
on shaded walls;
outside light filled the street.
The cloth and the fish
and the grapes were white
but the mariners were eating meat
and laughed and talked in a tongue I knew
but could not understand
for the blankness in my head.
Where now is your ship mariner
and what was it you said?

[Archive poem, 18 August 1943.]

Evergreen

The rustic hawthorn red and white
sturdy in the springtime light
is bumpkin nursemaid to young love.
Surfeiting with milky flowers,
she summons love with fragrance
and bids it go with thorns:
since then how many magic morns
have melted in the buttercups
amid the meadow sweet's decay?
I had forgotten till today.
Beyond cold lawns in sorrel set
and melancholy yew
and crazy pathways paved with pain
suddenly awake
I knew
the linden leaf is green again
to make
the new love old
the old love new.

[*The Irish Times*, 19 February 1944.]

Shutters

I have reaped my last harvest of pity
for all the disloyalties are I.
How pagan lovely through thin slits of thought
the ephemeridae of the turning shaft,
brief glimpse, brief sunlight that the
Brownian motes reveal,
limelight that never clove to avid mouth,
but pin point sang and danced
revolving in simplicity
of beam and mote and laughter inviolate.

[Archive poem.]

Insomnia

Tell them to go away:
last night Cuchulain slammed the gate five times
and hammered on the window panes,
and then his dog sat on the lawn
and howled and whined,
and after that a beggar banshee keened
and put the Ulster hound to shame.
I have not slept.
Then towards the dawn
strange workmen flickered saffron flags of flame
startling the shadows from their secret raths
to leap and bound about the walls,
and doffed the candle's silken hood,
the wick bereft was blunt and blackened as a clove.
They tapped and tinkered on the frozen pipes,
I heard their creak upon the cistern stairs
till in the peevish light
the clangour of the convent bell
like a ship staggering through clammy fog,
banished all phantoms and I slept.
Tell them to go away till noon
and I will bind in dreams the wraiths
that pilfered last night's sleep.

[*The Irish Times*, 4 May 1946.]

Stratosphere

The tension of the songs is now so high and thin
that only the dogs can hear it
and that is why they howl.
No one hears the sound of a leaf.
It is become a brutal thing
for the songs are high above.
The flowers tipple their syrup
on the harassed bee – like a drunk
without harmony.
Birds sing the harsh staccato of warning
giving substance to the glass silence
whose bitter shards
pierce the desolate ears of the dog.

[Archive poem.]

Clinic
(To Claire O'Mahony)

This morning a princess came
into the crowded clinic,
grave and pale and calm,
just five years old.
Her dark drooped lashes
masked her eyes,
but royal gold
new minted in her hair
trickled from a taffeta bow
to frame that pallid face.
The listless princess,
schooled to answer
vouchsafed a name
faintly but clearly as the chime
of tinkling wind glass stirred
on some soft summer day.
She was as old as vellum.
remote, restrained.
Disowned by father, dispossessed
of childhood's dynasty,
her foster mother's love disdained,
in dignity she walks a world defiled;
like bitter aloes in her lovely mouth
the arid lonely words – nurse-child.

[*The Dublin Magazine*, Vol. XXI, No. 3,
p. 5, July–September 1946.]

Song

The gipsy woman promised me
in a shower of petals
beneath a tree
my true love would wait for me
on the moonlit grass,
with a fairy coach
of sparkling glass.

But now I know
the petals in this icy snow;
strange lover in a black cockade,
of pine that trysting tree was made;
and dark the road we must traverse,
that crystal coach a lamplit hearse.

[*The Dublin Magazine*, Vol. XXI, No. 3,
p. 6, July–September 1946.]

Lullaby

Sleep, baby, sleep
While sleep is simple.
Frustration, only, opens your eyes
and the long discomfort of living
is still a vague surmise.

That idle trollop, the spinning moon
staggering round the empty skies,
like a drunken midwife, far too soon
wanted your coming,
glistening with pallid sweat she swoons.
Baby shut your eyes.

Rushlight will be your nightlight now,
but the moon will come back again –
stately and sober visitor,
impartial nurse to your newfound pain.

Sleep, little baby, sleep,
for the nightlight will grow so tall;
four white tapers around your bed
gossiping on your new linen shawl,
two at your feet
and two at your head.

There is no moon, for fog and damp
submerge the city
and giant cobwebs hang

from lamp to lamp.
The river out of pity
smuggles decently
its pauper cargo
shrouded in mist,
past the Customs
out to sea.

Each night the dragnets of the tide
take the shattered moon
beyond the harbour bar
but she reluctant suicide
nibbles her freedom and returns
to climb beside the nearest star.
One clear night endures her pain
to plunge to baptism again.

Sleep, baby, sleep
and sleeping thrive.
Your gentle mother
caught a mouse
and burned it on the hearth alive.

Sleep, baby, sleep.
They will give you toys
books and a rainbow to paradise
and two penny coins
to lay on your eyes.

Prolong your interrupted dream; postpone
the age distraught
when you will scour all zones
of street and thought
to find

false liberation for the mind
and fail,
joining the addicts whom
no drug can lull,
nor dream atone
when winter opens its grim jail;
lusting alone, for the soft cocoon
of death – to dull
the atrocious cancer of despair
that first bereaves the heart
and then the bone.

Sleep, baby, sleep
and do not cry,
you are so young
your eyes are dry.
You have no skill
yet to distil
the precious tears
silver handsel
of the sentient years.

Sleep now sleep
till through the snows
the crocus and the primrose break,
ancestors of those
who, for your sake,
will flower, one far off spring,
when you awake to love and know
the piteous lovely world
is in your power.

[*The Dublin Magazine*, Vol. XXII, No. 2,
pp. 1–3, April–June 1947.]

Untitled

The skull lies within my hands
the eyes are craters of past worlds
and worlds to come
and the skull is wounded;
let no rose grow in the clotted drops
not yet, although
the loins have leashed their burden
long ago.
Love a little for the nothingness,
the seed is sown;
for minute moments, let us live alone
and drink each other in a cup
that has no past or future to discuss,
but the living bone
that echoes like a seashell faintly blown
only for us — only for us.

[Archive poem, 12 February 1947.]

Frost

Tinsel rain
on the window pane,
blue snow
on the road below,
tangerine glow
from curtained casements,
the tenting of the sky swings low.

The washing on the line
that gaily frolics in burlesque
of owners demure or swaggering.
Wild bludgeoning of striped shirt sleeve
or flimsy frills of lace faint flickering
or merry romping children's frocks,
stout dish cloths or slyly dancing socks,
untrammelled sloughs exult
and flag the scarecrow, master of their cult
of saturnalian insult;
but suddenly grotesque
they freeze in tortured attitudes,
paralysed by Winter in their sin
and rigor mortis has set in.

[*The Irish Times*, 22 February 1947.]

The Charity

In flooded garrets icy cold
shivering and hungry mothers bore
their sickly infants, doomed before
they saw the light, both soon frail flotsam
on far Lethe's shore.
This is Dublin, till one valiant heart
moved by this misery and piteous loss
made himself champion of their part
soldier and surgeon, Bartholomew Mosse
with hands and brain and scanty purse, alone
transformed a vision into stone
and lit it with a purpose that has shone
across two hundred years,
till like a giant lighthouse
its broad beams reach
and compass all the world
to warn – to light – to teach.
Over dark Dublin's dirty streets
intrepid butterflies were borne,
jewelled heads and subtle fans
skirting the mire in tolled sedans,
laughing and lovely and gay,
beleaguered by beggars all the day,
for footpads caring not a jot,
careless that typhus kissed a beauty spot
or lurking Asiatic cholera leers,
soft clouds of powder puffed
from high piled wigs beneath the chandeliers.

Their veins ran red with claret
that some young cub
ravening from the Hell Fire Club
tapped in sport or sulky arrogance.
Huguenots spun their arts of France –
Poplins, satins but forsook
the Liberties to hang
the Ormonde gang
on their own butcher's hook.
They danced their dance until there came
Peelers and merciless gas light in rebuke
of watchmen, link boy, tawdry satin, soiled peruke.
Rutland the debonair was dead
and in his wake the brilliant swarm soon fled.
Now it was anaesthesia *à la reine*,
paved highways and the railway train
and great names rose to star
the lightening skies:
Labatt to cleanse, Collins to hear the unborn heart,
Macan to save the new born baby's eyes
and many more whose mighty ghosts
must press
round each new Master
when he consecrates his seven years
to women in distress
and watching bless
the immortal spirit that has passed
from the first Master to the last.

[*The Irish Times*, 12 July 1947. In July 1947 a Bicentennial
Congress in obstetrics was held in Dublin to com-
memorate the foundation of the Dublin Lying-in

(Rotunda) Hospital. This commemorative ode was spoken to mark the bicentenary celebrations of the Rotunda Hospital, Dublin, which took place two years after the event because of the Second World War. The British Congress of Obstetrics and Gynaecology was held in the Rotunda and in the Royal College of Surgeons and Physicians and was the first major post-war international conference.]

The Migrants

The curlews come out of the hearts of the dead
and cry on the brink of the flooded lands
driven to the parched, crying, crying
'have you forgotten the drowned and the damned?'
The wild geese searching their famished goslings
foundering in the mud,
the three swans wheeling
seeking their royal blood:
the wild birds, the magic birds
diving to death on the frozen mere
thrusting their desolate image
ghost voices shaking the air
in warning and fear,
the migrants bitter accusatory cry
'We want that you too might not die'
but some have starved and some
too loth to fly
have swilled in fat and sloth
and lumbering will never cleave
the icy sky.
Can they still hear
the souls lament; the bitter words
the famished utterance of the migrant birds.

[*The Dublin Magazine*, Vol. XXIII, No. 2, pp. 2–3, April–June 1948.]

December 1948

Lightening – the snap of purple satin
from the maypole of the universe,
a flicker in the auditorium –
heralds the buffoon's guffaw in late December,
when in this mildest month
the sparrows bud upon the brown fruit trees.
A painter's palette kills
a painter's knife
poignards the listening fields
and beauty born to madness dances,
only Saint Francis
weary of it all
counts the sparrows as they fall.

[Radio Éireann, 31 January 1949.]

Old Toys

Breathe quietly now, the dolls are asleep.
Old deaf and blind
and sleep is kind;
life still flickers like the seed of fire
in grey turf ash
that can be fanned to the fragile glow
of glimmering mind
and rosy speech that gladly sinks
deeper below
from earthly ill.
Wandering in quiet they do not dream:
the embers crumble,
the room grows chill,
mouth open, jaw relaxed, they give
the simulacrum of disordered death.
Stiff effigies, eyes gummed, but still they live.
Do not rouse them. Do not weep
these embryos of eternal sleep.

[Radio Éireann, 31 January 1949.]

The Chestnut Tree

The chestnut tree has thrown
her russet gauntlet down
and stark
but for her girded bark
watches in every street
and town
out-runners of the winter's dark,
the python fog, the stinging sleet.
Man-handled by the wind,
spat on by bitter rain,
she hears unsheltered feet
dispirited tread the glare
she flung for them.
The snow will wind her
shroud in vain,
for she through love
will live again.

[Archive poem, 11 November 1950.]

Vale (Alfred R. Parsons)

How praise this ardent life
this straight devotion, this learned anchorite
who taught the children
nursery rhymes?
Physician, chemist who had time
to see a troubled student's private pain,
scarce pausing his brisk tread
to leave his wisdom
in the anguished brain
as fodder for a foolish heart,
unheard by all his glittering train
of student satellites.
Dramatic teacher of the young,
first honesty he taught among
all other things.
'What? did you hear no murmur there?'
'You're sure?' 'Yes sir.'
A smile, and then
'Those who said none are right,
the others wrong.'
Old, but not full of years,
no failure there.
Ever alert of step, and ear and eye
we had forgotten he could die
and when he did, so live was he
confused, we wondered why.
His was the green old age of the god
that sadly watched a world decay.

Now the dark ferry paddles him away,
but as black Charon dips his blade
the god will say
'He is the immortal
I the shade.'

[Archive poem. Alfred Parsons (1864–1952)
was visiting physician to the Royal City
of Dublin Hospital, Baggot Street, and
an influential and highly regarded clinical
teacher for fifty-eight years.]

THE UNINVITED
A poetic drama

THE UNINVITED

A Play in One Act and Two Scenes

To A. J. Leventhal

DRAMATIS PERSONAE

Three Witches:
UNA
MIRABELLE
GRIMALDA

OLD NURSE
PRINCE
PRINCESS

Ancestors:
NUN
SAILOR
GAY LADY
TOREADOR
POET
PADDY THE MUC
CHILDREN

Others:
CAT
PARROT

SCENE I

A forest-glade. Lighted castle on hill in background. Two witches — Una and Mirabelle — in conversation.

UNA: Come, Mirabelle, our eagerness has pressed
us on too soon,
now let us rest
and wait the moon
and though the castle blooms with light,
topaz faceted against the night,
puzzling the fireflies with its saffron glow,
yet 'tis but right
these mortal guests should wait us
and humbly expectantly invoke
our presence there as fairy folk
bearing our precious gifts of magic,
so not too fast.
It would be tragic
if we were not last.

MIRABELLE: Yes, but did you hear a mew
as poignant as a child's first cry?

UNA: A mew? Not I —
                Our precious cats are fast asleep,
                warm and cosseted and far away.

MIRABELLE: But truth to tell
                I don't think Snowdrop
                has been very well
                throughout this day

(Enter Grimalda)

GRIMALDA: Well! I declare my two own sisters
                loitering, consulting there in whispers,
                adventuring like country maids in ditches,
                armoured in darkness — yet afraid.
                In sooth a sorry pair of witches!
                What tryst attends you in this glade
                that I should startle you.
                Or is the moon too new
                to gather herbs to brew
                some foolish potion
                designed to snare a village oaf's devotion?
                Rosemary, ragwort, rue and sage,
                dabbling in simples at your age,
                willows, like the local quack
                to cure the gnarled and creaking back
                of old rheumatics,
                since you both lack
                the brains to study mathematics,
                that cosmic key of wizardry.

UNA: Good heavens, here she is
                     and not in very festive mood:
                     when she is cross she can be very rude.
                     Have we no simple spell
                     to sooth her irritation
                     and so stop
                     this talk of education?
                     Yes! Snowdrop!
                     She's very fond of cats
                     and that's a lure she won't resist I'm sure.
                     (Eagerly)
                     Sister, Snowdrop is ill.
                     You know how delicate she is,
                     so highly bred, fragile as thistledown.
                     Advise me for my heart is smitten.

GRIMALDA: You know quite well
                     she is over-fed
                     — and probably in kitten.
                     A whey-faced, blue-eyed cat,
                     but truth to tell
                     most suitable familiar
                     Mirabelle,
                     Scorned of black warriors like my Lucifer,
                     a milksop and a sneak.

MIRABELLE: Indeed, Grimalda he was round last week!

GRIMALDA: Don't interrupt. It was not for her.
                     Of other things I wish to speak.
                     What are you plotting here,
                     old fashioned unhygienic crones?

[73]

I see no newts or herbs or dead men's bones.
Your brooms are fresh with flying ointment,
Where is the secret dark appointment?

UNA: Grimalda you are so quick and wise ...

GRIMALDA: At least I've learnt to use my eyes,
                and furthermore, thanks to my studies of
                    nutrition,
                kept them in excellent condition.
                You've never heard of vitamins
                and for your sins
                half-blind must peer and prowl
                from dusk, when I am dark-adapted like the
                    owl,
                and so this night will soon reveal
                what you are trying to conceal,
                with foolish chat
                about a cat
                (and such a stupid beast at that!).
                Well sisters, are you listening?
                You may as well confess
                your news.

UNA: We journey to a christening.

GRIMALDA: Whose?

UNA: The young Princess ...

MIRABELLE: A pretty babe with golden hair
                and heavenly azure eyes — like Snowdrop's!

GRIMALDA: All infants' eyes are blue
                 And so was Cyclops'
                 but she has two –
                 a nose, a mouth, four limbs;
                 the usual inventory to bind
                 the parents to her whims.

MIRABELLE: But little nails like rosy shells
                 and little fists so firm!

GRIMALDA: Here nothing premature, the child
                 must be full term.

MIRABELLE: You are so cold Grimalda,
                 and god-mothers are naturally excited.
                 We have worked so hard both day and night
                 to get the omens and the portents right.

Crackles of blue flame appear on the ground. She and Una look embarrassed.

GRIMALDA: This *feu de joie* has certainly gone wrong!

UNA: I *said* the brimstone was a little strong.

GRIMALDA: Idiots, who cannot learn a simple sum
                 But fooster dangerously by rule of thumb!
                 (to Una)
                 You're still conceited
                 for you once discovered
                 fox-glove for a failing heart
                 but overdosed a king.
                 And had he not recovered,

you would have learnt
your sole reward
in being burnt.

MIRABELLE: I hope the forest won't become ignited!

GRIMALDA: Much I care! I haven't been invited.

UNA AND
MIRABELLE: How could they have forgotten you?

GRIMALDA: Indeed! But none the less it's true.

MIRABELLE: We bring the baby health and wealth and
        beauty,
      as is our duty.
      But you?
      What will you do?
      You will not harbour spite
      against this helpless new-born mite?

GRIMALDA: No need for such alarm,
      the child herself I will not harm.
      But every family
      carries strange fruit
      within its tree
      that long coffined in the glossy wood
      dreams in the sap for centuries of birth,
      waiting the kinsman's kiss
      to set it free in flesh
      to putrefy the earth.
      The young Princess's lot

will be
to carry fruit.
Like me —
forgot.

UNA AND
MIRABELLE: We do not understand.
                  You say you wish the Princess well
                  and yet you talk as if you planned
                  some curse, some evil spell?

GRIMALDA: It is the future I foretell.
                  Now go! and I will quench
                  these crocus fires of puzzled spring,
                  these phantoms ... To the palace bring
                  joy and laughter now, forgetful of the stench
                  that hallows birth and heralds death,
                  the baptism of blood, the ring
                  of toadstools that invade the dying breath,
                  the brief delay
                  between
                  the pristine green
                  and verdigris decay.
                  Oh! go away
                  and leave me here
                  to see in darkness clear
                  the things that lie beneath my lids
                  addled by light, but like the grids
                  of Spanish convents, shutting out the day.
                  What, still here?
                  I suppose you have forgotten how to steer
                  your half-anointed brooms.

Fortunately it is not far
or you would spend the moon in some high
    tree.
(*Points*)
Look Mirabelle, *this* is the star
and fireflies to light you through the gloom.
(*Picks fireflies up*)
If you would not set your sticks alight,
take off away from here –
and now good night.

Exeunt Una and Mirabelle. Grimalda waits and listens.

CAT: Miauw!

GRIMALDA: Lucifer my own!
                  Come for at last I am alone.
                  Lucifer marauding son
                  of Satan,
                  what have you done?
                  Triumph is strangled in your throat,
                  you come as warriors will,
                  seeking praise for what you kill,
                  and I will praise you whether
                  it is bat or mouse or rat – but no! – a feather
                  celestial blue, no common tit or royal
                      peacock this,
                  a fragile bird whose death is swift, whose
                      song men bless,
                  blue bird of vagrant happiness.
                  This is the official bird of state.
                  Well better kill it now than wait.

[78]

Wise cat to bring me such a treasure!
I will dissect it at my leisure.
When happiness grows cold
it is the proper study of the old.
Dear cat, whose Egyptian god demands
the best of sacrifices,
your grateful priestess understands
and this suffices
for the insults of this vacant night
that torment wisdom and vaunt delight.
Lucifer king and emperor of cats
whose lineage is strong to breed,
whose seed
carries no dotage, whose greed
is dominant, making a faithful image of itself,
smothering the white cat's kittens who are
    deaf,
but alas!
powerless to pass
this mighty heritage to your black stalwart
    sons,
you are unique.
But they
some day when wrongly mated may
beget a freak.
See I will stroke your velvet ears
until you purr
my Lucifer
and in the witch ball
we will watch
what happens after twenty years.

From out of the folds of her dress Grimalda produces a crystal after she has spoken the final three lines or during the speech. There appears on a possible screen or front curtain a circle which expands and finally with the drawing of this curtain exposes Scene II.

SCENE II

The sleeping beauty in her bedroom inside the castle. The castle disappears with the drawing of the first curtain. Enter an old nurse with a broom.

OLD NURSE: Well Princess, still asleep?
                    The young drowse deep,
                    but this outspans the normal dream
                    that blurs the senses
                    while the rising sap
                    trickles from heart to finger tip,
                    to eye, to rosy lip.
                    Well, let these cobwebs stay
                    until mayhap
                    you wake one day
                    and break this soft cocoon,
                    this filamentous tomb
                    spun on the loom
                    of dreaming mind
                    to find
                    the hour of gold,
                    the hour of birth to life –
                    and from that hour
                    grow old.

[81]

Who would forswear
that hour for this? *(Points)*
Trance that but waits
a lover's kiss.
Did she die now,
the sundial could not mark
her coming or her passing
since they both are dark.
Her breath
but wantons in her breast,
so deep her rest,
its fickle flight would scarce attest
her death.
(Exit)

Enter children dancing. Children might wear clothes suggesting ballet.

CHILDREN: We are tired of sleep and now we want to
       dance
       because we have so little chance
       of ever being born.
       We are the silent satellites
       of bridal rites.
       We are the recessive genes
       suppressed by adult dominants.
       We cannot die but shuffled fly
       from troupe to troupe.
       We say good-bye
       to our weak comrades,
       crying *'auf wiedersehn'*
       for should we meet again
       in different bridal train

we will embrace and in twin sympathy
be borne as one.
That would be fun!
That would be fun!
We have so very little chance but there is one.

They repeat the refrain. One boy drops out and lies down.

FIRST CHILD: What ails the little boy
                 he is so pale and short of breath?

SECOND OLDER
CHILD: Oh! yes, you see he always
                 bleeds to death.
                 He must do this when we rehearse.

FIRST CHILD: I hope he won't get any worse!

SECOND CHILD: Oh! No he only shows his taint.

FIRST CHILD: It seems to me the girls don't faint!

SECOND CHILD: They are the clever ones who slyly
                 pass it to their sons.

FIRST CHILD: That is not fair!
                 Is the mother without love
                 to bear
                 a child to such great trouble?
                 Has she not known?

SECOND CHILD: Some do and some do not

and some don't care.
The ignorant disown
their ancestry,
deeming themselves victims of a plot.
They call their 'scape goat 'changeling'
and to appease this wizardry
burn the babe upon a red hot shovel.

FIRST CHILD: I'm glad I am recessive
if words in the world mean such a lot.
While we are unborn here we need not feign
innocence, nor suffer pain.

SECOND CHILD: But hush! Our superiors
arrive – the Kings and Queens.
Recessive we cannot strive
against these lordly dominant genes.

(Enter Nun clapping her hands)

NUN: Now children you've had your play
and recreation's over.
Quick now run away!
Don't stand there arms akimbo!

FIRST CHILD: Where do we go?

SECOND CHILD: Oh! Just back to limbo.

NUN: Hurry I'm going to ring the bell.

(Takes hand bell out of her pocket)

FIRST CHILD: Well, I suppose it's worse in hell.

SECOND CHILD: They cannot send us there
                no matter how much they may desire.
                Unborn we bear
                no mark of Cain
                and knowing not pain
                we could not feel the purge of fire.

Nun rings bell. As children bow, curtsey and run off, enter Gay Lady, Toreador, Poet and Sailor. Last has parrot on his shoulder and is dressed like a romantic pirate. They bow formally to each other. Other indeterminate characters volonté *drift in. They, too, bow.*

SAILOR: How does our sleeping beauty?

NUN: Still heedless of her duty,
                while we, her ancestors, must pace
                the corridors of time that she alone
                can fashion into space,
                giving our spirits flesh in birth
                to walk and work again on earth.

SAILOR: Aye, but the girl does not know this.
                Strange that a life should hang
                upon a kiss.

GAY LADY: Sailor, how many careless kisses
                have you given?
                No need to blush dear man
                for here you're shriven.
                Birth waters wash away all knowledge.

Only the instincts then remain,
so you would do the same again.

NUN: You should not bring that parrot in.

SAILOR: Why not? He saw a living parrot in a cage
and fell into a fearful rage
and claimed his ancestral right
to follow it, and I was loth
to leave him for we hope
that birth will re-unite
us both.
This parrot is a sage.
Why once he said ...

GAY LADY: There sailor, keep the bird
but I don't believe that he can speak.
He hasn't uttered one small word.

SAILOR: Excuse me M'am but he,
(Deeply hurt)
in company of fools,
n'er opens his beak.

TOREADOR: Shame on the nobles
who leave such beauty undisturbed
for years! No serenade,
no carnival, no rose! absurd!
Ah! Were I not a shade ...

CHARACTER: There rides this way a Prince,
(From wings)
his horse caparisoned in leaping gold!

GAY LADY: Swift! The others must be told,
             should it be he at last!

CHARACTER: Gold and silver and he travels fast.

(Exit)

NUN: I dedicated my life to God,
             gave my beauty as a peerless pearl
             and now once more I pray
             life to renew my vows
             of sacrifice to serve
             the divine eternal spouse.

GAY LADY: Foolish girl!
             Why anticipate
             inexorable fate?
             This mystic union
             that you crave
             awaits you in the
             sacramental grave.
             A necrophile to pray for life!
             To cherish in the heart of youth
             the loathsome worm decay.

TOREADOR: Nay! The nun is right I say.
             Death is the hour of truth
             and blood the baptism of death
             as it is of birth.
             Life's dignity lies in valour
             ardently pursuing
             to conquer death by wooing.

[87]

What man on earth
would craven die in bed
when the bull challenges
the horns of truth upon his lowered head,
when choice is chance
and skill and fear are dice
to lose or gain
the victim of the welling stain
that soaks the ring?
Eyes glaze and in that sweltering heat,
I know not whose.
In the hush I wait
the crowd's great roar.
If 'tis the bull they are reprieved,
if 'tis I, they lose
and will be grieved
and I will hear that sound no more.

Enter Prince who is attracted by the beauty of the Sleeping Princess, and who is unaware of other characters on the stage. Children come dancing in.

CHILDREN: The Prince, the Prince!
                Now is our chance
                to dance, to dance ...

Repeat refrain from 'we are the silent satellites'.

Hymn of Ancestors — spoken in chorus by all the characters except of course Prince and Princess:

We who have lived and still sustain
our substance in your cells

beg to be born again.
The life urge now compels
us to this portal,
in surging siege,
to storm this citadel
to make us mortal.
Our crusade is fratricide;
appeal to reason is denied.
Love our pitiless liege
so darkens all the mind
that they are deaf
as well as blind.

POET: This is the spiritual hour
when tear drops tremble on the rose
and music is a tremulous call
to greater love, to immolation
in gratitude for revelation,
when May thorn blossoms shower
confetti from a blackened tree;
untarnished, chaste, supreme,
the vision widens as the lovers dream.
Alms for the world they leave bereft!
Wine for the guests and sacrifice of self!
The charity of love is great but brief,
for time the thief
folds up his glimmering tapestry,
silent, swift and deft.
Softly the dream world shrinks, for he is
    nimble.
The guests are gone, the lovers wake.
All that is left

is love incarnate as a symbol.
The earth
is richer by a birth,
for better or for worse
the universe
may now disperse.

Prince kisses Princess who wakes.

Enter Paddy the Muc who is revoltingly ugly and dirty, and might wear the mask of a pig. He carries a goad.

PADDY THE
MUC: (*Addressing the Ancestors*)
                Hold! Do you hope to keep me out?
                I, Paddy the drover,
                beast of all beasts — a lout
                they say and worse,
                whore-master, pitiless and cruel,
                maimer of neighbours' cattle,
                driving parched animals with goad and curse
                to brutal slaughter, to feed with blood
                my swollen purse.
                What foolish woman's prattle!
                When the red gold of coin can buy
                the king's own daughter;
                and what does the gentle shepherd do
                but raise his tender flock for slaughter?
                Hypocrisy! Incest, murder, rape?
                These are but naked words and I'm a man
                and fearless, needing no cape
                to veil my violence, only my two strong fists
                    to grip

and wring each second's bargain
from the flying hour
and god-like grow in wealth and power. Power
is my lust—the sense and smell of it;
but it is torture that exults me most
that sets me free to stride and boast
and sweat with ecstasy –
warm sweat that laves my armpits and my
    groins
and seals my navel's hoarded dirt
when it congeals ...

NUN: (*Raising her rosary*)
             Demon!

GAY LADY: (*Brandishing her fan*)
             Obscene!

SAILOR: Unclean!

TOREADOR: (*Gesture with sword*)
             Scarce worth steel!

POET: *His* wounds would heal.

PADDY THE
MUC: Back, back you snivelling pack!
             (*To Nun*)
             You, whey-faced wimpled simpleton,
             back your beads to tell
             in the half-lit world
             of a convent cell;

miser of life who hoards
talents to trade for death's rewards!
(To Sailor)
Back sailor, who would squander
precious life to wander
and ship-wrecked sell
this gift for a shifting bed
of jagged coral shell.
(To Gay Lady)
And you who would frivol life away
in charming play
of make believe.
(To Toreador)
And you who cannot wait to die
but swagger thinking to defy
the canker that gnaws without reprieve:
black rose no blood will stain to red.
Children all, who cry
for something priceless, as a toy,
and granted it, first flaw and then destroy.
While you pursued the shadows
of yourselves,
I lived in every thought and deed,
lavishly I sowed my seed.
The lovers plight their troth
but *I* am ancestor of both
and by this double might
I claim my right!
Back, back everyone!
I Paddy, am their destined son.

By this time Paddy the Muc has driven off all the Ancestors. The Prince and Princess, unaware of all the confusion, continue their mime of court-ship throughout the scene. They now prepare to leave hand in hand and move towards exit back stage followed triumphantly by Paddy the Muc.

(*The Dublin Magazine*, Vol. XXIV (New Series), July–September 1951.)

SUGGESTED READING

Adams, B., *Denis Johnston. A Life* (Dublin: The Lilliput Press, 2002).

Coakley, D., *Oscar Wilde: The Importance of Being Irish* (Dublin: Town House, 1995).

Collins, L., *Poetry by Women in Ireland: A Critical Anthology 1870–1970* (Liverpool: Liverpool University Press, 2012).

Craig, G., Fehsenfeld MD, Gunn, D., More Overbeck, L. (Eds), *The Letters of Samuel Beckett, Vols 1–4* (Cambridge: Cambridge University Press, 2016).

Cronin, A., *Samuel Beckett: The Last Modernist* (London: HarperCollins, 1996).

Knowlson, J., *Damned to Fame: The Life of Samuel Beckett* (London: Bloomsbury, 1996).

Lyons, J.B., 'MacCarthy, Ethna Mary' in McGuire, J., and Quinn, J. (Eds) *Dictionary of Irish Biography* (Cambridge: Cambridge University Press, 2009).

O'Brien, E. (Ed.), *A.J. Leventhal 1896–1979: Dublin Scholar, Wit and Man of Letters*, Leventhal Scholarship Committee (Dublin: The Glendale Press, 1984).

O'Brien, E., *The Beckett Country: Samuel Beckett's Ireland* (Dublin and London: Black Cat Press & Faber and Faber, 1986).

O'Brien, E., *The Weight of Compassion & Other Essays* (Dublin: The Lilliput Press, 2012).